THE STATESMAN

THOMAS WRIOTHESLEY, THE FOURTH EARL OF SOUTHAMPTON

BRYAN DUNLEAVY

THE STATESMAN

THOMAS WRIOTHESLEY,
THE FOURTH EARL OF SOUTHAMPTON

BRYAN DUNLEAVY

Published by the Titchfield History Society 2023

ISBN 978-1-915166-08-1

www.titchfieldhistory.co.uk

A catalogue description of this book is available from the British
Library

THE STATESMAN

There was something about the destiny of the Wriothseleys in that they did not live long lives. The second earl was only five years old when his father died at the age of 45. After a brief majority he died at the age of 36, leaving an eight year-old heir. The third earl did better, and could have looked forward to another decade at least, but in 1624, caught up in one of the Duke of Buckingham's pointless military ventures, he died of dysentery In Holland at the age of 51. Worse still for the earldom, his eldest son, James, had also died of camp fever only five days previously. So it was that his second on Thomas found himself the heir to the earldom at the age of sixteen.

This immediately created another minority situation, although thankfully for the Southampton estates, not as long as it had been for his father and grandfather. Nevertheless, the economic impact was immediate. The two life annuities of £3200 each that had been awarded to the third earl were suspended immediately upon his death, as well as the life interest in Lyndhurst manor. The new era could no longer count on the profits of office that his father had enjoyed as thee would now go to another's benefit. For the next five years the young earl was under wardship, the profits of which were granted to the duke of Buckingham. In addition the king's third of 3400 a year had to be paid out of the estate plus £2000 to the Crown for the wardship and marriage of the young earl. In 1629 the dowager Countess had to pay a further £234 for the earl's livery. The situation was further complicated by the absence of any will from the third earl. Fortunately for the Southampton family, King Charles' sister, the Empress Elizabeth, was a good friend and was able to intervene to resolve the situation favourably.

Thomas, born in 1607, was the fourth child in the family. Penelope was born in 1598, Anne in 1600, James in 1603, and Elizabeth in 1609. The family was later completed with the birth of Mary, whose burial was recorded in the Titchfield Parish Register 10 January 1616.

The baptism of Thomas Wriothesley was recorded in a most unusual place. Little Shelford in the county of Cambridge has this record:

> 1607 Thos Wryosley S. Henry and eliz. Wryosley. Erle and
> Countess of Southampton, baptised 2nd April.

The village is far away from any Wriothesley landed interests, which were concentrated in Hampshire and London, and as far as we know, no land in Cambridgeshire was ever of interest to the first earl of Southampton. That the earl and countess were living there is not quire as quixotic as it first appears.

During James' slow journey from Edinburgh to London in 1603 he stopped over at Royston in Cambridgeshire. While there he was entertained by Robert Chester at his Priory House. The area struck the king's fancy and in the following year he rented Priory House and used it for his passionate pastime of hunting. Later he purchased two inns at Royston and converted them into a Royal hunting lodge, which he returned to every year. He was even there in January and February 1625, shortly before his death. In 1603 Southampton was now in favour after a decade in the political wilderness and he could scarcely run the risk of losing this important gain. It was therefore essential to be near the king at all times.

Fortunately, a suitable house was available for lease. Sir Horatio Palavicino (c. 1540-1600), an Italian born Anglophile who had many business dealings in England had built a splendid house in the Italian style. It was modern and palatial but Sir Horatio's son had little use for the property and was prepared to consider a lease. The mansion was an ideal property for use during the hunting season. They must have used it with some regularity, year after year. The industrious Mrs Stopes also uncovered evidence that two of Southampton's servants, John Cooke in 1608 and Valentine Metcalfe in 1615, had recorded burials in the Little Shelford register. This indicates that the house was in regular use and on a long lease, which may have concluded with the death of Henry Palvacino (Sir Horatio's son) who died in 1615.

We know practically nothing about Thomas's childhood. As a second son he would not be subject to the same expectations as his elder brother nevertheless, we can only assume that the two boys, close enough in age, grew up together, probably with the same tutor.

ROYAL VISITORS

The new king in 1625, Charles I, was also a second son, and was a man by temperament and by training unsuited to the role, as he amply demonstrated over the next quarter of a century. He was in thrall to the charming and adventurous Duke of Buckingham, who was no friend to the 3rd Earl of Southampton.

After the failure to secure a marriage alliance with Spain, Charles returned to England, and for the only time in his life, to popular applause, such was the relief in England that the marriage would not go ahead. He would never again enjoy such popularity, as he set on a course of intransigent adherence to his own will. He never fully understood popular opinion in any case, nor was he sensitive to many of the courtiers closer to him. He was an extremely introverted man who constructed a carapace of self-belief around himself. Strong monarchs of the past knew the time to be resolute and understood that there were moments to compromise or make concessions.

Charles never had that instinct; he was a weak man who believed that his adamantine refusal to deviate showed strength. As described in the previous chapter, the collapse of his Spanish marriage proposal turned him, without much thought, to France for a replacement bride. A French princess, Henrietta Maria, was offered on condition that she was able to maintain her catholic faith in a protestant country. This was agreed, although at some cost to the English, as Charles and Buckingham agreed to commit 6,000 troops to the Dutch war of independence. Buckingham believed that he had Richelieu's support to reclaim the Palatinate for Charles' brother-in-law, but when he returned to France to stand in for Charles at his wedding to Henrietta Maria he discovered that Richelieu had no such intention of wasting French resources on a war that had no interest for the French. The commitment of troops to to the Dutch war in 1624 proved to be a wasteful exercise, not least because it cost the lives of the third earl and his eldest son.

The new queen, after her proxy marriage, travelled to Titchfield in an echo of that other fateful queen, Margaret of Anjou, who came to Titchfield Abbey in 1445 to marry Henry VI. So the new earl found the new king and queen on his doorstep at Titchfield in August 1625. The Parish Register has left this record.

King Charles and Queen Mary came to Titchfield place the xxth day this month and the Queen stayed there five weeks and three days.

Royal visits were expensive and a mixed blessing. They conferred prestige on the host and good hospitality might lead to future favour, but they were often ruinously expensive. Five weeks was a very long stay, but, after eating the earl and his countess mother out of house and home, the new king and his wife eventually left for London. Why the king chose to stay at Titchfield is not known; there were other great houses near to Southampton which could have accommodated the king's entourage. The old earl had died the previous year and the new earl was a minor with no influence. There were no obvious political advantages for the king, but none may have been considered. The land route up the Meon Valley to London was easier than some of the alternatives and this may have been the deciding factor.

One might have expected some favour to fall on the Southamptons after their pleasant hospitality, but such warm feelings appear not have been in the make up of the introverted Charles. He was a thoughtless man. His assumption of what was his by right took no account of any sacrifices made by others and his general insensitivity to this was to characterise his kingship. He was not driven by malice in this instance: he was an inward-looking man, largely oblivious to the feelings of others. He could by no means, for example, be compared to the malevolent Mabel de Bellême, an 11th century French countess who deliberately descended on an abbey with her retinue and made sure that they used up all the abbey's provisions before leaving, as punishment to an abbot who had upset her. However, the actions of the king, and their consequences must be noted rather than the motivation behind them.

RESPONSIBILITIES

Once free of the burden of hospitality to the royal couple the new earl was able to get on with his life. Still three years shy of his majority, he had little authority in the administration of his estates; in any case, they could be competently managed by the stewards and the countess. He was free to plot his own course. He seems to have determined in the first instance to enter St John's College, Cambridge to complete his studies. Edmund Lodge, writing in 1838, says that he went to Eton and Oxford. The Eton College Register records his attendance from 1617-1619. Oxford may be discounted as there was never any connection between that university's colleges and the Wriothesleys. He is on record as having attended St John's College at Cambridge and as this was the Alma Mater of his father this makes sense. He was certainly at St John's in the Michelmas term of 1625 when he was 18, an age which would have made him older than other undergraduates. This was a year after the death of his father and brother and leads one to wonder if this might be a voluntary act on his part, possibly sensing some deficiency in his education. Perhaps he had studied there a few years earlier.

He finished with St John's in 1626 and there is no record of the award of a degree. He then decided to travel to France, a sensible enough way of filling the time before he could take control of his inheritance. His sojourn would broaden his education and enable him to make contacts that might be of future value. He came to like it and although he retuned to England from time to time to take care of business he did not return permanently until 1634. He effectively 'dropped out' of English society for eight years and was content to leave the day-to-day management of the estates to his mother and their stewards, dropping in every now and then to give direction where it was needed. In retrospect this seems to have been a remarkably cool-headed decision. He had not been schooled to take over as earl; that had been the destiny of his older brother James. He must have known within himself that he was not ready. In any case he was a young man with a few wild oats to sow, and there is evidence that he shared his father's taste for gambling; far better to do that away from the prying and disapproving eyes of the English court and his family retainers.

This decision caused him to be absent from the political fray, which was beginning to become increasingly polarised in England. In retrospect, although he may have thought nothing of it at the time, he was able to bring some balance and detachment to his political counsel when he did enter the lists in 1640 as a mature man.

For most of his reign Charles favoured other interests over those of the 4th earl. Principal among them was George Villiers, Duke of Buckingham, who had captivated King James and continued to work his charm on his son. He was no friend to the Southamptons and enriched himself at the expense of the two earls on more than one occasion. Buckingham was a reckless adventurer who led his compliant monarch into several foreign policy fiascos. In 1627 Buckingham led an army to the port of La Rochelle on the west coast of France in order to assist the Huguenots who were in rebellion against Louis XIII. The ill-prepared and poorly disciplined invading force was no match for the French and many lives were lost. The Huguenots and the remnants of the English forces were pressed into the walled town, where they lay under long-term siege. Buckingham was entirely blamed for the failure and he became the most hated man in England. So much so that when he was assassinated in Portsmouth of 23 August 1628, his murderer became a popular hero. This rejoicing was evident in the village of Titchfield when the man responsible for the Parish Register wasted little time before recording this unnecessary this entry:

> The Lord Duke of Buckinghame was slayne at Portsmouth the
> 23 day of Auguste being sattersday Generall of all the fleete by
> sea and land whose name was George Villiers Right Honerable.

The assassin was John Felton, a former officer who had some personal grievances against Buckingham. Buckingham was staying at the house of Captain Mason in Old Portsmouth High Street. The house is still there. Felton had travelled down from London fully intent on his deed and after breakfast on 23 August he stepped forward to the unguarded duke and plunged a knife into his chest. Felton's last words to the duke were, "May God have mercy on thy soul!" Felton made no attempt to escape and was eventually tried, sentenced and hanged, but not before receiving applause as a popular hero.

In one sense the duke's untimely death would have removed one obstacle from the progress of the House of Southampton. However, the king had a low emotional intelligence and instead of seeing the assassination as a signal that he should modify his policies, simply doubled down on his old entrenched position. One optimistic view, expressed on the day after the assassination, "the stone of the offence being removed by the hand of God, it is to be hoped that the king and his people will now come to a perfect unity."

The hope was entirely fanciful. When Parliament opened in January

1629 Charles embarked on a collision course with the assembly on the role and power of the church. A century after the break from Rome England was now a Protestant country and nothing, short of invasion and conquest, would turn the country back. Charles' attempts to Romanise the English church met with stiff resistance. After a showdown and the imprisonment of leading members, Charles dissolved Parliament. It was not to be called again for eleven years.

Earl Thomas was at this time largely removed from such quarrels. He came into his majority in this year and. apart from occasional visits to England, was enjoying life in France.

Coming to Grips with Reality

The earldom was at a financial low point. The great estate built up by the first earl hd been put at risk, at first by the extravagance of his son, and then by the youthful indiscretions of his grandson. It is to the credit of the young fourth earl and perhaps a testament to the resilience of the original portfolio, that matters could be corrected. His father had left heavy debts and the wardship had enriched the duke of Buckingham without addressing the debt issue. In addition, the widowed countess was entitled by law to one-third of the estate. Earl Thomas began on an immediate sale of land. Walsworth was sold for £1900. The house, manor and rectory of Dogmersfield fetched £3600 and the sale of the Itchell and Ewshott manors brought in a further £3000. Further sales of two manors in East Horsley, Surrey that he had inherited from a great aunt in 1626, together with West Men and a manor in Lincolnshire raised a further £19000.

The sums raised were enormous but only went part way in dealing with the debt burden. He was able to redeem property that had been conveyed to Arthur Bromfield (the earl's steward) in 1611 for £20,000 and pay some debts with the remainder. Even so, he was still under pressure and in 1633 was considering the sale of the Beaulieu estate. Fortunately the sale of trees in Titchfield great park to the navy in 1633 came to the rescue. This brought in £2295. He had also taken out mortgages in 1630 to the sum of £3,000. These were paid off in 1641 through the sale of Soberton and Flexland to the bishop of Winchester.

This was much to the credit of the earl; however, he also inherited some of the headstrong traits of his father. He was a gambler and was attracted to horse racing. Almost inevitably he suffered losses and in n1634 he sold his stud to pay these debts and set off for France.

Marriage

There he met and fell in love with Rachel Massue de Ruvigny, from an aristocratic Huguenot family. Despite sensible advice to the contrary, he married her, even though there were both financial and political negatives to the marriage. He had been offered the hand of the daughter of Sir Thomas Thynne of Longleat with a very handsome dowry of £40,000, yet, just as his father had spurned a marriage to Lord Burghley's daughter and suffered a heavy financial penalty for his refusal, so did Thomas Wriothesley follow his father's instinct. The marriage did not sit well with the French catholic wife of Charles I, Henrietta Maria, who could not in conscience tolerate the

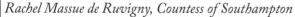

Rachel Massue de Ruvigny, Countess of Southampton

Protestant Huguenots. Thus, Southampton put his political career at risk.

Rachel and Thomas were married at Charenton in France on 18 August 1634. She was very beautiful but brought no dowry with her. Almost a year later, on 6 June 1635, she gave birth to a son, who was named Charles. He was not a strong child and he died a few months later on 20 November. A second child, this time a daughter, Elizabeth, was born a year later. She later married Edward Noel, the 1st earl of Gainsborough, and became one of the inheritors of the Southampton estate. A second daughter, Rachel, was born in 1637. She first married Francis Vaughn who died in 1667. There was no issue from this marriage and she remarried William Russell, the second son of the earl of Bedford in 1669, at the age of 32. The dukes of Bedford descend from her. Another son, Henry, was born in 1638, but he died 4 years later. Countess Rachel died on 16 February 1640, while giving birth to a fifth child. The child did not survive either.

Two years later, earl Thomas remarried, this time to Elizabeth Leigh. She bore four daughters, but only one survived. She was named Elizabeth like her half-sister and she later married the first duke of Montagu.

Out of Royal Favour and In

The earl's lack of favour at court left him vulnerable to Charles's predatory taxation policies. In 1635 Charles set up a commission to review the boundaries of ancient royal forests and the earl became an easy target. The Crown decided the 2,236 acres of land at Beaulieu was royal forest, and the earl's complaints and appeals against the decision fell on deaf ears.

The earl spent the first decade of his majority rising his family and restoring his estates to good order. He was remarkably successful. He held no offices at court, where he was out of favour, and could focus entirely on bringing his own estates into good order. In this he demonstrated intelligence and creativity. The traditional approach to leasing land was for the lessee to pay a fine on entry and thereafter a low rent. Southampton transformed this policy by setting a low entry fine, or sometimes none at all, and charging a higher rent. One example is a Beaulieu farm which had been leased at £10 per annum with a £50 entry fine in 1616, was renewed in 1639 at £20 per annum with no entry fine at all. The consequence of this policy was that he considerably increased his revenue. So, although he had to sell of about a quarter of his estate after 1629 to pay his father's debts, his rental income in 1642 on the remainder of his Hampshire property was £2700 - £300 a year more than it had been in 1624!

Loyalty

In 1639, at the age of 32, earl Thomas was still outside government. Charles was faced with another potential invasion from Scotland and like an early medieval king sought to raise his army by feudal means. All of the peers of the realm were commanded to meet the king in York with their retinues. Mercenaries were also raised in the Midlands to complement this force. They were not fighting men and were leaving their work as plough-men and bakers without any military experience. It must be assumed that the men assembled by the peers had some training but many were reluctant and it is quite likely that they recruited men who equally lacked enthusiasm. Men raised from Hertfordshire in particular refused to be conscripted and fought against their officers before returning home. Conscripts from other parts of the country pillaged villages and tore down enclosures which had appeared in recent years. Some opened up the gaols to free prisoners. Those with a religious axe to grind attacked and looted churches. After a decade of direct rule by the king his oppressed people were in no mood to risk their lives for a royal cause.

It must be assumed that the earl of Southampton dutifully raised a force of men despite difficulties. As a relatively benign manager of his estates he would have no difficulty in calling on his supporters. In addition, he would not have been among those lords who were by this time in direct opposition to Charles. The king now demanded an oath of allegiance from all the lords. Lord Brooke and Viscount Saye refused to take the oath unless it was approved by Parliament, which of course was not possible since Charles has disbanded that institution ten years earlier. Charles responded by arresting the two men and sought to charge them with treason. He was then advised that Brooke and Saye had broken no law; they had merely asked that Parliament approve the oath, so Charles was obliged to back down.

The military activity went no better. One force sent out against the Scots retreated at first sight of a superior army. The Scots in the meantime were careful not to attack while they knew that the English forces were not supportive of their king. They waited while Charles depleted his treasury and came to a truce of sorts in July.

The king eventually had to concede that he could not cope alone with the Scottish problem and grudgingly conceded to advice to recall Parliament. Elections were held and the new Parliament assembled on 13 April 1640. Southampton would have been amongst those Lords. If Charles imagined that appeals to fight for king and country would be sufficient to gain the endorsement of Parliament he was in for a surprise. All of the grievances of the previous eleven years, the ship money tax, the monopolies, the extension of royal forest laws now tumbled out in speech after speech and Parliament wished that these issues could be addressed before tamely agreeing to raise a tax to subsidise the king. The king put forward his request five times in slightly different forms but each time the Commons either demurred or rejected the proposal. On 5 May, having achieved nothing, Charles dissolved Parliament. It is known to history as the 'Short Parliament'; it achieved nothing but to set the country on a path to civil war.

England was clearly a divided nation and the Scots seized their opportunity. The Scottish army crossed the River Tweed in July and occupied Northumberland with no resistance. Charles set out from London with his army on 20 August 1640 and from York sent out an army to repel the Scots. The two forces met at Newburn and the English retreated ignominiously after the first shots were fired. Hardly any Englishmen, it appeared, was willing to put his life on the line for this unpopular king. The news of the defeat was greeted with celebrations in London; presumably other parts of the country, after a decade of royal monopolies and unjust taxes felt the same. It must have been obvious to wiser heads that the king had lost his own country.

Charles then summoned the peers of the realm to York and for the second year in a row the earl of Southampton made the journey to York. Their advice to the king was that he should recall Parliament in order to agree a peace treaty. Charles resisted at first but with the Scots demanding sums of money that only Parliament could approve, Charles bowed to the inevitable. His experiment in ruling like an Angevin king was over.

The news was greeted with joy in the country as people were generally optimistic that the restoration of Parliament would bring back the country to normalcy and send the Scots back across the border. But the scars left by the summary dissolution of the 'Short Parliament' remained and. if anything, those elected to the Commons were more belligerent and steadfast in opposing the king than before. Grievances had piled up and the House of Commons, under the leadership of John Pym, still wanted the king to address them. The new Parliament, known to history as the 'Long Parliament,' took up the cause which had been so rudely interrupted in the Spring and Charles was now in a much weaker position and forced to make concessions. One rumour that made things worse was the belief that Charles would bring troops from Ireland to England to restore order. This was known as the 'army plot' and the king's chief advisor, the unpopular Thomas Wentworth, Earl Strafford, was implicated. Strafford was the leader of those who encouraged the king in his hard line policy. He was a doomed man, but of interest here is that only two peers refused to agree to the Commons protest about the army plot or to the attainder of Strafford. One of them was Southampton, who was firm in his principles. According to Clarendon he had 'a particular prejudice' against Strafford, whom he saw as badly advising the king; nevertheless, he did not allow personal dislike to overcome his principles. Strafford was accused of treason and many of the charges were trumped up. Obviously Southampton saw through that and was prepared to stand up for what he believed to be right. In reality it was the king's policies and his inflexible attitude that enraged the Commons and Strafford was in many ways a surrogate target. Charles could have saved him from execution, but that would have meant making concessions. So Strafford went to the scaffold and nothing was resolved.

Parliament did agree to a payment of £300,000 to the Scots, but only after a number of concessions from Charles. The puritanical faction in

A portrait of Charles I with his son James.

Parliament, having tasted power, began to press for more, and this had the effect of pushing more moderate voices, such as the earl of Southampton, in to the royalist camp. Moderate voices, naturally enough, were critical of the king's policies, but at the same time had no interest in a revolution which would mean handing the government of the country to Parliament. The effect of Parliament's more extreme proposals during this year was to push people, who had hitherto not supported Charles, into the royalist party.

One outcome from this latest debacle was that Charles belatedly recognised the worth of Southampton as a supporter, and after years of neglect, appointed him gentleman of the bedchamber on 30 December 1641 and made him a Privy Councillor a few days later on 3 January 1642. This may have been one of his wiser appointments. The earl was intelligent and diplomatic but he was no mere yes man.

And indeed he was (according to Lord Clarendon) a reluctant convert to the king's cause. Charles had granted no favours to Southampton during his 15 year reign and might have been considered hostile to the earl's interests, as we have described.

Southampton emerges during this period as a man with a gift for statesmanship. This in itself is remarkable. After spending his twenties living in France and the period after 1634 restoring good management to his estates, he was a very late entrant to the political world. But his voice was listened to from the first. He must have had impressive gifts. Once he cast his lot with the monarchy he stuck to it out of firmly held principle. He afterwards accompanied the King to York and to Nottingham, and was present at Edgehill. His counsel was always to seek peace and compromise and after the king raised his standard in June 1642, Southampton advised him to talk to the Parliamentary side. Eventually, and after running out of other options, Charles agreed and he sent Southampton together with Edward Sackville, Earl of Dorset, Sir John Culpepper and Sir William Uvedale to carry the message of "his constant and earnest care to preserve the public peace."

Charles was not believed, but he did at least understand that Southampton was respected by the other side and kept Southampton for any peace-making role over the next few years. Southampton was one of the commissioners who tried to negotiate the Treaty of Oxford (Feb-Apr 1643). In January 1643 Parliament asked for talks. The king agreed and the Parliamentarians came forward with the same proposals they had put to him in York in June 1642. The king's commissioners received them and there was a delay until March when the Parliamentary commissioners were allowed to return. The negotiations did not go well and were frustrated by Charles' prevarications and changes of mind. Even though there were extremes on both sides, there was potential for a compromise. Such a proposal, supported by Clarendon and Southampton, was to shelve the issue of the abolition of bishops and to skirt round Parliament's objection to the king's control of armed forces by appointing the earl of Northumberland as Lord High Admiral. The queen scuppered this as she detested Northumberland, so these negotiations ended in April with no agreement. In any case, Queen Henrietta Maria had just landed from the Netherlands with money and reinforcements and with the prospect of winning a battle the king had no incentive to compromise.

The next round of negotiations were conducted at Uxbridge between 29 January and 22 February 1645. They were tripartite, with representatives of Parliament, representatives for the king and representatives of the Scottish government. Southampton was one of 19 commissioners for the king. Once again the talks proved to be fruitless as both side felt that their military forces had been strengthened.

In this assessment the Parliamentarians were proved right. The two armies met at Naseby in Northamptonshire on 14 June 1645 and the New

Model Army won a decisive victory. The king was still not ready to recognise this reality and it was not until 20 June 1646 that he was eventually willing to surrender. For much of the Civil War Oxford became the temporary capital for the king. London was hostile and although the citizens of Oxford were not supportive, most of the colleges were. The city was placed under siege three times during the Civil War and it was only after the third in 1646 that Charles capitulated. Southampton was one of the privy councillors who signed the articles of capitulation.

Clarendon made this comment about his friend Southampton's dedication: "although a person naturally loving his ease, and allowing himself never less than ten hours' repose, he was then never more than four hours in bed; bending his whole soul towards effecting an union which he never ceased to consider as the greatest blessing which could befall his afflicted country."

After that, Southampton played no active part in the war, choosing to abide by the articles he signed. The same could not be said for Charles who, as ever, was looking for ways out of the predicament he had largely created for himself. The earl held to a principled position; he had agreed to and signed the document of June 1646 and the matter was therefore closed. His decision also turned out to be a prudent one; after the war many royalist supporters were heavily fined, but Southampton seems to have escaped such punitive measures. It would appear that Southampton was respected by the Parliamentarians even though he ended up on the losing side.

Southampton still had one part to play in the last years of Charles reign. Charles was kept under house arrest at Hampton Court Palace, but one November night in 1647 he slipped away from Hampton Court with a small party. They rode through Windsor Forest and reached Farnham in the early hours of the morning, 12 November. From there it was the intention to proceed to Bishops Sutton. near Alresford, and from there make their way to the Isle of Wight, where Charles believed that he had sympathisers. He may also have intended to escape to France. However, they learned that Bishops Sutton was occupied by Parliamentarians and there was a change of plan.

The main party was to continue to the Isle of Wight, while Charles and a single companion diverted to Titchfield, where the fourth Earl of Southampton could be counted on to accommodate him. Thus it was that Charles returned to the house where he had honeymooned with his young bride 22 years earlier.

Robert Hammond was Governor of Carisbrooke Castle and the Isle of Wight at this moment. He had served in Cromwell's New Model Army

The rooms at Carisbrooke Castle occupied by Charles I.

and was ranked as Lieutenant Colonel. Charles believed that Hammond was sympathetic to the royalist cause and had charged his men with negotiations. Hammond realised that this put him in a very difficult position but agreed to travel with Jack Ashburnham, one of the king's close attendants, to meet the king at Titchfield. There he explained that he was in no position to assist the king with his escape plans but he was prepared to offer him safe custody at Carisbrooke Castle. The king felt that Hammond could be trusted to act with honour and agreed to accompany him back to the island. Thus began a long period of incarceration for Charles, from 13 November 1647 to 29 November 1648. The king was at least safe from the extremists, the levellers, who would have no compunction about taking the king's life. Cromwell was probably content to have the king tucked away from active interference in government, but Charles, incorrigibly, continued with his secret manoeuvres with both factions of the army and the Scots. He contrived to sign an agreement with the Scots which guaranteed the establishment of of Presbyterianism as the state religion. In return a Scottish army would march to London to enforce 'a full and fair parliament.'

Several efforts were made to reach an accommodation with Charles but he persisted in actions to destabilise the state and eventually Parliament settled on a final solution. It took almost two months of argument to bring everything to a conclusion, possibly an outcome that few wanted, but made inevitable by events, the beheading of the king on 30 January 1649.

Southampton was among the few peers permitted to attend the trial of the king. Following the king's execution, he obtained leave to stay in the palace of Whitehall, where it is said that he witnessed Cromwell approach Charles's corpse, consider 'it attentively for some time', and then mutter the words 'cruel necessity'. Finally, Southampton attended the king's funeral at Windsor on 8 February.

One has to admire Southampton's steadfastness to the idea of kingship. He was not alone; the overwhelming majority in the country understood monarchy to be the only effective way of running a government, and in the 17th century they were probably right. Government by Parliament was the solution of dreamers and could not work, as Oliver Cromwell soon discovered when he had to assume the role of a king without the title. There was nothing in Charles's behaviour towards the earl over a period of 24 years that could cause the earl to love him, in fact, as we have seen, Charles sometimes behaved very badly towards him. Nevertheless, loyalty to the anointed monarch was a principle he would never discard.

THE WILDERNESS YEARS

Parliament's treatment of Southampton's estates was relatively lenient. In November 1645 the committee for the advance of money had assessed him at £6,000, although there is no evidence that this sum was ever paid. In the autumn of 1646 he begged to compound under the Oxford articles and was assessed at the rate of one-tenth, or the value of two years' income from his estates, and on 26 November his fine was set at £6,466. In the autumn of 1648 the Commons confirmed his composition fine and ordered him to be pardoned for his delinquency and the sequestration to be taken off his estates. We do not know if this fine was ever paid, and thereafter the committee for compounding apparently ceased to pursue him.

Even so, the Civil War and its aftermath did some harm to the South-ampton estates. £980 worth of iron was seized from the Beaulieu furnace and wood to the value of £235 was cut down, and, as earlier mentioned, there was damage to the new buildings at Bloomsbury.

After the king's execution Southampton lived in retirement in Hamp-shire. Although the council of state kept an eye on him, his political activities were extremely limited throughout the 1650s.

His only political intervention during these years was to offer assistance to the young Charles II, to whom he remained deeply loyal. He played no part in the forlorn attempt to overthrow the Parliamentary regime but after the battle of Worcester in October 1651, he sent word from Titchfield that he had a ship ready for Charles. The king had already secured a boat to take him to France but he 'ever acknowledged the obligation with great kindness, he being the only person of that condition who had the courage to solicit such a danger'. After the king's escape Southampton 'had still a confidence of His Majesty's restoration'.

Earl Thomas had signed an agreement with Parliament in June 1646 and he intended to honour it and until the Restoration in 1660 he remained politically inactive. He did not for a moment deviate from his belief that the Parliamentary regime was illegitimate, but he determined to remain neutral – he would neither support nor work against the new regime. Various overtures were made to bring him on side but he rebuffed each of them. There was even an occasion when Cromwell was in the New Forest and thought to visit him. The earl got wind of this and arranged to be unavailable.

Southampton was never a career politician. As already noted, he steered clear of political activity until 1642 and then exempted himself after 1646. He responded twice to calls from his king to bring his talents to government, the first to bring his counsel to Charles I at his moment of desperate need, and the second, to be discussed in the next chapter, to take high office for Charles II at the Restoration. In both cases he was a reluctant recruit whose only motivation appears to be a willingness to act out of a sense of duty. He was a rare man.

The only time he got into trouble was when he took a stand on a matter of principle. Parliament had assessed a decimation tax in November 1655. Southampton claimed that this violated the Oxford articles under which he had surrendered in 1645 and refused to give particulars if his estate. He was briefly imprisoned in the Tower, but released shortly when Parliament realised that they did not have legal case in this instance.

THE RESTORATION

On the Restoration of the monarchy in 1660 Southampton was one of the first to be called into the new government. Time had made him something of a rarity. In 1660 he was one of only two who had ever served the king on the Privy Council on a list of 70 presented to Charles II when he reached Canterbury. Charles had no difficulty in accepting him. His loyalty to the crown was unquestioned and he was also a man of great ability. He was immediately appointed to the Privy Council and made a Knight of the Garter. On 8 September he was appointed Lord Treasurer, an office he was to hold with distinction until his death. He was not in the least tempted by the opportunities for peculation and corruption, a fact that was noted in his day. 'He was an incorrupt man, and during seven years management of the Treasury he made but an ordinary fortune out of it'

He came to an agreement with the king that he would take a fixed salary of £8,000. This was a large amount of money, but in comparison with conventional practice this represented a model of restraint, a practice not emulated by the king and many of his courtiers who continued to waste money for their own pleasure. He did try to warn the king that 'the revenue is the centre of all your business', but his caution went largely unheeded.

In government, he tried to become a voice of moderation. He argued for magnanimity towards the king's opponents and against replacing one extreme with another. The military government of Cromwell had led to excesses by the authorities and he felt the new regime would be better advised not to follow the same path.

Charles II continued in the manner of Stuart kings by being profligate with public money. In some respects he was worse than his straight-laced father. He had great need of a man like the earl who could raise sufficient money for domestic extravagances and foreign adventures, such as wars with the Dutch. Earl Thomas had a hard job. Parliament was generally reluctant to raise taxes and the Stuart expedient of loans, used by both Charles I and Cromwell, became a great headache for the Treasurer. He complained to

Charles II.

Pepys:

> 'What will you have me do? I have given all I can for my life.
> Why will people not lend me their money? Why can they not
> trust the king as well as Oliver.'

Pepys was struggling to find money for the navy on the occasion of recording this exasperated remark to pay sailors in the navy and he was having to deal with riots. He concluded that the solution was either 'money or the rope', realising that the second option was the only long-term solution. Earl Thomas could only sympathise and was clearly frustrated at his

Edward Hyde, Earl of Clarendon.

relative impotence. The unspoken answer to Southampton's questions was that Oliver Cromwell held one card that Charles II could not play - the threat of execution!

Earl Thomas was now in his fifties and had little inclination for such frivolities; he was ready for the serious work of government. His continued friendship with Clarendon was a factor in ensuring that his advice was heeded. Clarendon, as Lord Chancellor, was the most powerful man in government.

Edward Hyde was almost an exact contemporary of Thomas Wriothesley, being born at Dinton in Wiltshire in February 1609. He was also a younger son so like his friend he grew up with no expectations of inheritance and would have to make his own way in the world. He also shared with Thomas the fate of succeeding to his father's estate through the early deaths of brothers - in Hyde's instance two elder brothers. His original destiny was to take orders in the Church of England; instead, he redirected his study to law at the Middle Temple. He had considerable intellectual abilities and he was an excellent public speaker, and after being called to the bar in 1633, quickly established a thriving practice.

Hyde was first elected to the Short and then the Long Parliaments in 1640. He was initially critical of Charles, but as a moderate could not countenance the extreme reforms of many parliamentarians and therefore placed his support behind the king.

After the royalist cause was lost in 1646, he went into exile in Jersey. Like Southampton, he did not approve of Charles' underhand dealings with the Scots that led to the second civil war of 1648. During the next decade he wrote his History of the Civil War.

Charles II appointed him Lord Chancellor and he held that office until 1667 and in that respect his time in high office mirrored that of his friend Southampton. Soon after the Restoration he was made Baron Hyde and in the following year Viscount Combury and the Earl of Clarendon.

Edward Hyde became the dominant figure in the new government but two other men, Sir Edward Nicholas and James Butler, who became the 1st Duke of Ormond, became principal secretaries to the king. Together with Southampton, this quadrumvirate, formed a core council to the king. New men, who came over from 'the other side' and had been instrumental in the Restoration joined the council.

As Lord Treasurer, Southampton had the key role financing government and given the unfortunate relations between the earlier Stuart kings and Parliament, this was by no means an easy challenge.

The third earl, in the first two decades of the 17th century, started to pay attention to this development. Southampton House grounds were first taken up for shops and houses. In 1613 the earl began to lease lots for building on the Bloomsbury manor and in 1616 he purchased part of the manor of St Giles in the Fields for £600, which enabled him to further extend his frontage along Holborn. The rentals from Holborn and Bloomsbury were starting to inch upwards in 1624 but even so only accounted for 6% of all estate rentals.

The fourth earl continued the development of Bloomsbury which he had started in the 1640s. First he had built Southampton House for his own occupation, a large mansion on a site called the Long Field. After the restoration and with new income at his disposal he could afford to build on a grand scale. In the open space on the south side of his house on Great Russell Street he created a piazza in the Italian style. It was known as Southampton Square, although today it is called Bloomsbury Square. In the crowded cityscape of London this square must have been a delight. An 18th century drawing by John Stow, shows the grand Southampton house and the square to the south, with elegant terraces on either side. The square is crossed by diagonal paths as well as paths through the middle. Samuel Pepys described this small suburban town as 'a very great and noble work' after he visited in 1684.

This whole area between the city and Westminster was completely transformed by the developers in this century. That intrepid horseback traveller and diarist Celia Fiennes (1662-1741), left her observation of this development at the end of the 17th century;

'There was formerly in the City the houses of several noblemens with large gardens and out houses . . . but of late are pulled down and built into streets and squares and called by the names of the noblemen.'

During these years there was a dramatic rise in income from the Bloomsbury manor. Bloomsbury was not a rental property in 1601 and in 1624, when the fourth earl succeeded his father, the annual income from rental was £22, little more than a small country manor. By 1668 this income had risen almost 100 fold to £1,980. A century later, in 1765, this had increased to an astonishing £7,800. The Dukes of Bedford, through the marriage of William Russell to Rachel Wriothesley, became the beneficiaries of this, and their income today from their London properties must be astronomical by comparison to the 17th century. The seed of this great wealth was planted by the first Earl of Southampton.

In some respects the earl's long period out of public office was a great

Southampton House and Bloomsbury Square in an engraving dated 1754.

advantage to the development of the estates. When he inherited in 1624 the estates were still encumbered by debt and his father had largely survived on generous pensions and sinecures from the crown. These sources of revenue dried up in 1624 and the new earl was forced to live within his means. He proved to be creative and astute, and, largely due to the Bloomsbury and Holborn development, had recovered the family fortune at his death. He only held public office for about 4 years in the 1640s and for the last years of his life from 1660.

William Wriothesley, Sir Thomas Wriothesley (1st earl) and Henry Wriothesley (2nd earl) lived short intense lives. The longest lived of those three was Thomas, who died at the age of 45. The third earl was set to live longer but died of dysentery in 1624 at the age of 51. Thomas, the 4th earl, stands out as the only male to live to almost 60 years. Towards the end of 1666 he became gravely ill and after a lingering illness he died at Southampton House on 16 May 1667. After his death they cut open his body to reveal an enlarged kidney and a large stone in his bladder. He endured his final months with considerable stoicism. Samuel Pepys reported that he prepared himself for the end by 'closing his own eyes and setting his mouth, and bidding Adieu with the greatest content and freedom in the world.' Pepys could identify with the pain the earl. must have felt as he himself had suffered from an enlarged bladder stone. The pain became so excruciating that at the age of 25 he submitted to an operation without anaesthetic whereby iron forceps removed a stone 'the size of a tennis ball.'

As Pepys left Southampton House he discovered the porter in tears. No doubt the emotion was genuine, but Pepys was a practical man and reasoned that his opportunity for tips was much diminished by the death of his master: 'he hath lost a considerable hope by the death of his Lord, whose house will no more be frequented as before.' So Pepys gave the man a large tip and it was probably the last time he had occasion to visit Southampton House.

The body was prepared and taken to Titchfield where he was buried on 18 June 1667. The parish register made this record:

> June the 18th 1667 Then Buried Thomas Ryothizley Eirle of
> Southampton High Treasurer of England to Charls the 2

Earl Clarendon had this to say about his friend and colleague. 'He was a person of extraordinary parts, of faculties very discerning and a judgement very profound.'

He was the most statesmanlike Wriothesley since his great grandfather and namesake. The third earl, his father, had many gifts but was prone to being erratic and quarrelsome. His grandfather effectively exempted himself from any consideration at court by his uncompromising position on religion. All of these Wriothesleys were highly intelligent men but it was the fourth earl who understood the virtues of accommodation and compromise.

Lightning Source UK Ltd.
Milton Keynes UK
UKHW050835030123
414745UK00002B/9